DARK OCEAN STRATEGY

THANAKRIT **LERSMETHASAKUL**

Dark Ocean Strategy
by Thanakrit Lersmethasakul

© 2019 BlackBlankBlock

Publisher: BlackBlankBlock
www.blackblankblock.com
contact@blackblankblock.com

KDP ISBN: 9798679891470 (Paperback)

PREFACE

The purpose of this book is to apply the "Describe Less, Think More" or "DLTM" [1] principle, facilitating a meeting point between the author's ideas and experience sharing and the readers' imagination and implementation.

PREFACE

In contrast to other literature that merely provides ideas, solutions, or tools, this book goes beyond by integrating DLTM principles, simplifying communication, fostering synthesized thinking, and generating significant conclusions.

PREFACE

What do you know? and what you should know about the business situation or living environment around you? Here lead you into thinking inside a comprehensive analysis framework for every context, situation, and environment.

HOW TO USE THIS BOOK

"Describe Less, Think More"

Titles/Chapters

Ideas/Information

Questions/Practices

Core Concepts/Content

Description | Linkage | Highlight | [Reference]

INDEX

0. FROM AUTHOR	6
1. INTRODUCTION	7
2. VUCA WORLD	26
3. COLORFUL OCEAN AND STRATEGY	56
• RED OCEAN	59
• BLUE OCEAN	62
• GREEN OCEAN	65
• PURPLE OCEAN	67
• WHITE OCEAN	68
• BLACK OCEAN	69
4. DARK OCEAN AND STRATEGY	70
5. CONCLUSION	100
6. REFERENCE	101

0. FROM AUTHOR

Numerous individuals have shared their ideas, and through questioning and orchestration, I have formulated a strategic way of evaluating and managing several situations known as ...

Dark Ocean Strategy

http://www.Thanakrit.net
Lersmethasakul@live.com

1. INTRODUCTION

*"**Management** is doing things right; **leadership** is doing the right things."*

Peter Drucker

> "*Management is <u>efficiency</u> in climbing the ladder of success; leadership determines whether the ladder is leaning against the <u>right</u> wall.*"
>
> Stephen Covey

The overall management relates to <u>strategy</u> because determining the strategy is a critical decision to involve a significant commitment of resources, and once initiated, it is very difficult and costly to change.

Leadership is a potent combination of <u>strategy</u> and character.

" A vision without a **strategy** *remains an illusion."*

Lee Bolman

> "The essence of strategy is **choosing** what not to do."

Michael Porter

" Success is 20% skills and 80% strategy. You might know how to succeed, but more importantly, what's your **plan** *to succeed?."*

Jim Rohn

" Strategy is style of thinking, a conscious and deliberate process, an intensive implementation system, the science of insuring future success."

Pete Johnson

A strategy is a plan for the whole **organization** or an **individual**.

Strategic planning and decision making have an important role in development and <u>sustainability</u>.

A variety of <u>factors</u> drive organizations or individuals to adopt strategies in order to emerge successful such for instance is <mark>value</mark>, <mark>efficiency</mark>, and <u>effectiveness</u>.

When value includes being _profitable_, effectiveness may refer to growth and stability.

Value The monetary, material, or assessed worth of an asset, good, or service	**Efficiency** Managing the whole resources to meet objectives
Growth The expansion of transaction, execution, and collaboration	**Stability** A consolidation strategy, often before a period of growth

To assess value regarding something is held to deserve or **worth**, it is necessary to ...

- Determine
- Succinctly describe
- Quantify
- Model the values

The crucial **metric** for proving efficiency is ...

how close you can deliver bug-free products or services to your customers.

Successful growth strategies are based on having the resources to support growth, identifying the right targets that make growth worthwhile being better in **competition**.

Stability needs to establish clear procedures and **systems** during this period before moving on.

Survival is essential to most organizations or individuals staying alive in a highly competitive environment.

They have to be able to evaluate and manage several situations in the VUCA world.

What do you know about the business situation or living environment around you

?

2. VUCA WORLD

"<u>I know</u> your eyes
in the morning sun.
<u>I feel</u> you touch me
in the pouring rain.
And the moment that
you wander far from me.
<u>I wanna</u> feel you
in my arms again ..."

How Deep Is Your Love –
Bee Gees

We live in a world that's <u>constantly changing</u>, becoming <u>more unstable</u> each day, where historical forecasts and past experiences are losing their relevance and are becoming <u>more unpredictable</u>.

It's becoming nearly impossible to plan for future success as it becomes increasingly uncertain where the route is heading.

Problems and their repercussions are more multi-layered, harder to understand. The different layers intermingle, making it impossible to get an overview of how things are related – and deciding the single correct path is almost impossible.

"One size fits all" and "best practice" have been relegated to yesterday –

in today's world, it's rare for things to be completely clear or precisely determinable.

What you should know about the business situation or living environment around you ?

In real life or corporate life, the fast-changing environment and people lifestyles are demanding regular <u>situation analysis</u>, which is defined as an analysis of the internal and external factors of a business/life,

==to define current position== with a snapshot of where company/personal life is placed in the business/living environment, ==to find out== what ==the opportunities== should be actions to progress further, and also ==to forecast the results== if a decision is taken in any direction.

When considering a business situation, it is important to look at several factors that identify <u>business</u> capabilities and environment such as:

- <u>Product situation</u> related to your core clients' needs
- <u>Competitive situation</u> and advantages
- <u>Distribution situation</u> including intermediaries
- <u>Environmental factors</u> impacting business performance
- <u>Opportunities and issues</u> affecting business performance

The <u>Integrated Enterprise Architecture</u> [2] presenting business dimensions/factors for identifying capabilities and environment:

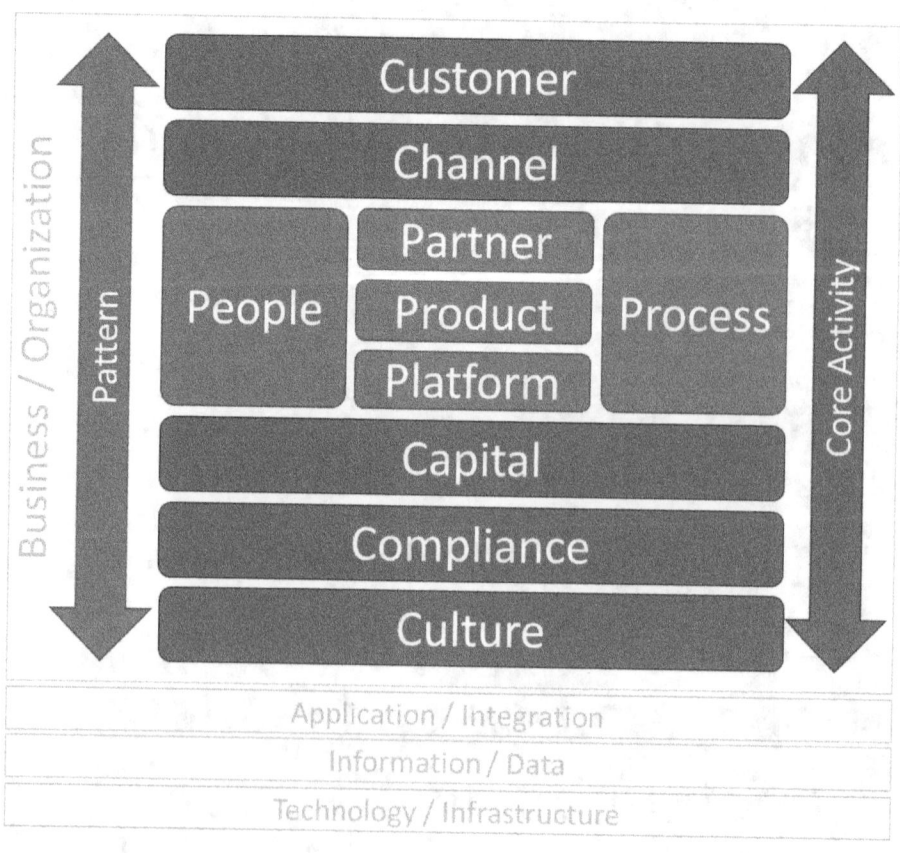

When considering a living situation, it is important to look at several factors that identify <u>life</u> capabilities and living environment such as:

- <u>Career situation</u> related to your workplace
- <u>Competitive situation</u> and advantages
- <u>Networking situation</u> including relationship
- <u>Environmental factors</u> impacting your performance
- <u>Opportunities and issues</u> affecting your performance

The Integrated Life Architecture [3] presenting life dimensions/factors for identifying capabilities and environment:

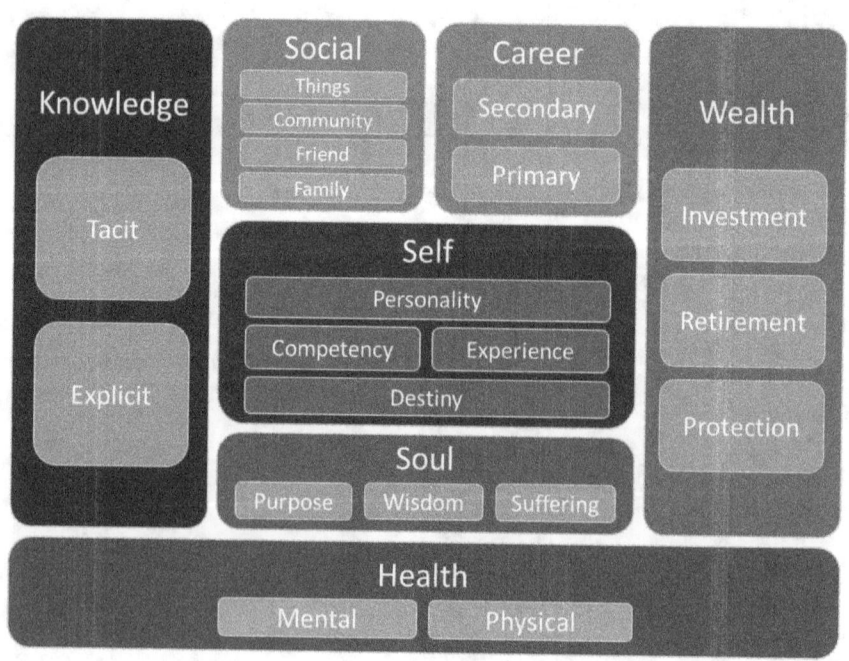

The <u>business/living environment</u> is created by combining the influence of <u>social</u>, <u>technological</u>, <u>economic</u>, <u>ecological</u>, and <u>political</u> activities which induce peculiarities as well as constantly change due to the continual evolution of these interlinked activities happening over time and space.

A situation analysis is an essential part that should be reviewed periodically to ensure that it is current.

VUCA is an acronym to describe or to reflect on the **Volatility**, **Uncertainty**, **Complexity** and **Ambiguity** of general conditions and situations.

Volatility

Volatility refers to the quality of frequent, rapid and significant change.

	Level of predictability of action results	
Complexity	**Volatility**	
Ambiguity	Uncertainty	

Level of understanding situation

Volatility

Volatility is often calculated using variance and standard deviation. The standard deviation is the square root of the variance.

$$\text{Volatility} = \sqrt{\text{Variance}}$$
(in a period)

Uncertainty

Uncertainty refers to the extent of the situation, in which future events and outcomes are unpredictable.

	Level of predictability of action results	
	Complexity	Volatility
	Ambiguity	**Uncertainty**

Level of understanding situation

Uncertainty

A measurement or calculate some quantity from data, It generally assumes that some exact or "true value" exists based on how they define what is being measured (or calculated). The results usually specify a range of values that they expect this "true value" to fall within. The most common way to show the range of values is:

Measurement = Best Estimate Uncertainty

Complexity

Complexity refers to factors that need to take into account, their variety and intricately interconnected.

	Level of understanding situation	
Level of predictability of action results	Complexity	Volatility
	Ambiguity	Uncertainty

Complexity

Any context of complexity is concerned about how fast particular calculation or process performs. It can be defined as a numerical function T(n) - time versus the input size n. and T(n) does depend on the implementation. For example, the time function T(n) using the quadratic time complexity "big-O" to express the complexity of a situation.

$$T(n) = O(n^2)$$

Ambiguity

Ambiguity refers to a lack of clarity and the difficulty of interpreting exactly what the situation is.

	Level of understanding situation →	
Level of predictability of action results	Complexity	Volatility
	Ambiguity	Uncertainty

Ambiguity

Ambiguous data or situations can be translated into structural restraints. In many applications, the required accuracy leads to a need for integration that becomes a challenge for real-time processing. The nature of ambiguity processing is interpreted and minimizes the processing burden without affecting performance.

What does VUCA mean to your **leadership** and your **strategies**?

CHAMPSPACE [4]

Living as a ...

Champion

=

Happiness

+

Success

CHAMPSPACE [4]

Strategic Characteristics for Success

Strategic Characteristics for Happiness

Challenge / Change
Holistics / Heuristics
Alchemy
Metaphor
Perseverance / Platform

Sufficiency / Simple
Patience
Attitude
Cause / Consciousness
Ethics

VUCA and CHAMPSPACE

In the context of leadership, VUCA strategy comprises **Vision**, **Understanding**, **Clarity**, and **Adaptability**.

VUCA and CHAMPSPACE

Vision

Paint a picture of the future you want

VUCA and CHAMPSPACE

Understanding

Understand interconnections; make them transparent

VUCA and CHAMPSPACE

Clarity

Focus on simplicity, what counts and what it's really about.

VUCA and CHAMPSPACE

Adaptability

Promote a culture for making decisions and accounting for mistakes. Facilitate innovation and build up resilience.

3. COLORFUL OCEAN AND STRATEGY

" Blue, green, grey, white, or black; smooth, ruffled, or mountainous; that <u>ocean</u> is not silent."

H. P. Lovecraft

Various types of strategies are used in strategic management such as ...

- Red ocean strategy
- Blue ocean strategy
- Green ocean strategy
- Purple ocean strategy
- White ocean strategy
- Black ocean strategy

These strategies are used in organizations by top level executive managers for organizational sustainability and to face or deviate from the competition.

Red Ocean

Red ocean strategy supports to compete in existing market space, beat the competition, exploit existing demand, make the value/cost trade-off, align the whole system of a company's activities with its strategic choice of differentiation or low cost.

Red Ocean

Red oceans represent all the industries in existence today in the known market space. In red oceans, industry boundaries are defined and accepted, and the competitive rules of the game are well understood. Here, companies try to outperform their rivals to grab a greater share of existing demand. As the space gets more and more crowded, prospects for profits and growth are reduced.

Red Ocean

Red Ocean Strategy consists of either cost leadership or product/service differentiation strategy.

Blue Ocean

In blue oceans, demand is created rather than fought over. There is ample opportunity for growth that is both profitable and rapid. There are two ways to create blue oceans. In a few cases, companies can give rise to completely new industries. But in most cases, a blue ocean is created from within a red ocean when a company alters the boundaries of an existing industry.

Blue Ocean

Blue ocean strategy supports to create uncontested market space, make the competition irrelevant, create and capture new demand, break the value/cost trade-off, align the whole system of a company's activities in pursuit of differentiation and low cost.

Blue Ocean

The basic ideas used for the Blue Ocean Strategy can be summarized as ignoring competition, creation of new markets, focusing on new customers, and value innovation.

Green Ocean

Green Ocean Strategy is a strategy to gauge the impact of environmental footprint on human lives. it is a hybrid mechanism which combines the best things that characterize Blue ocean and Red ocean strategies. The keyword in discussing this theory is sustainability and there can be no one-size-fits-all formula governing the innovation mechanism of an organization.

Green Ocean

Green ocean strategy is the strategy of sustainable development under the guidance of harmonious belief by increasing core and sustainable competence.

Purple Ocean

A mix of Blue and Green

White Ocean

White Ocean concerns about "social" more than "profit" that made it outstanding than the others oceans which is gaining reputation and profit from customer. The concept of White Ocean Strategy is focusing on People, Planet, Profit and Passion. Concerning in sociological and environment are most important in this ocean.

Black Ocean

Black ocean strategy is a kind of survival strategy to foresee the organizational problems and solve them successfully to continue in its business market by means of a kind of black magic may be legally or illegally, ethically or unethically.

Black Ocean

It is a smart strategy to ensure win in market place and continuing business.

Black Ocean

Black ocean strategy is not formulating strategy to face the competition by identifying various forces which affect the organizational business, it is not a method of developing monopoly product/service or identifying uncontested market space or a new way of serving the customer but it is a way of either killing the competitors, or creating a monopoly or solving life-threatening problems that arises due organization's own mistakes, or due to any environmental factors which makes the organization.

How **dark** is your life/business

?

4. DARK OCEAN AND STRATEGY

" The price of light is less than the cost of darkness."

Arthur C Nielsen

Dark Ocean

Dark Oceans represent **VUCA Intensity Level (IL)** of existing situations such as Red Ocean, Blue Ocean, Green Ocean, Purple Ocean, White Ocean, and Black Ocean.

Dark Ocean

VUCA Intensity Level (IL)

=

Volatility Level

+

Uncertainty Level

+

Complexity Level

+

Ambiguity Level

Dark Ocean Strategy

Dark Ocean Strategy (DOS) represents a strategic way of evaluating and managing across several situations and strengthen generic competitive advantages as well as unfair advantages for business sustainability.

It also can be used in conjunction with various types of strategies including ideas to implementation [7].

So, the best strategic question here to integrating **value**, **growth**, **efficiency**, and **stability** for organizations or individuals should be ...

What is the worth metrics and systems thinking for competitive advantage in the VUCA world ?

Metrics

The dimensions used in common assessment for comparing and tracking performance in general:

- Leadership Dimension
- Time Dimension

Metrics

The dimensions used in common <u>assessment</u> for comparing and tracking <u>business performance</u> for <u>any oceans</u>:

- Success Dimension
- Purpose Dimension (Business)
- Environment Dimension

Metrics

The dimensions used in common <u>assessment</u> for comparing and tracking <u>individual performance</u>:

- Success Dimension
- Purpose Dimension (Individual)
- Environment Dimension

Metrics

The dimensions used in common <u>assessment</u> for comparing and tracking <u>performance</u> for <u>the Dark Oceans</u>:

- Situation Dimension

Metrics

Success Dimension:

- **Value**
- **Efficiency**
- **Growth**
- **Stability**

Metrics

Purpose Dimension:

For Business
- Production
- Satisfaction
- Competition
- Relation
- Distribution
- Performance based on elements of Integrated Enterprise Architecture

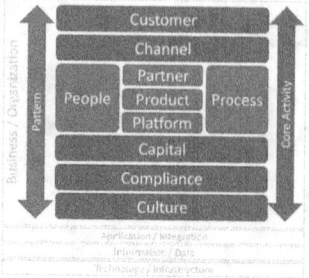

Metrics

Purpose Dimension:

For Individual
- Education
- Satisfaction
- Competition
- Relation
- Performance based on elements of Integrated Life Architecture

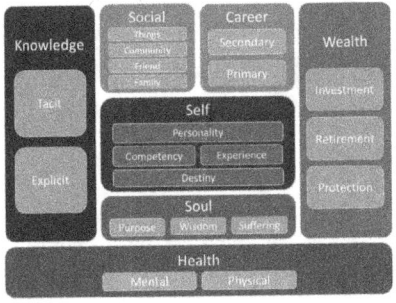

Metrics

Situation Dimension:

- **Volatility**
- **Uncertainty**
- **Complexity**
- **Ambiguity**

Metrics

Environment Dimension:

- Social
- Technological
- Economic
- Ecological
- Political

Metrics

Leadership Dimension:

- Vision
- Understanding
- Clarity
- Adaptability

Metrics

Time Dimension:

- Analyzing past transaction
- Defining current position
- Finding current opportunities
- Forecasting future results

Systems Thinking

One of all thinking capabilities [6], which help to leverage other thinking capabilities, is how to think holistically and focuses on the way that a system's constituent parts interrelate and work.

Systems Thinking

A strategic tool, supporting "How to think", linking inputs as a system called "<u>Blank Block</u>" [5] may be used for situation analysis.

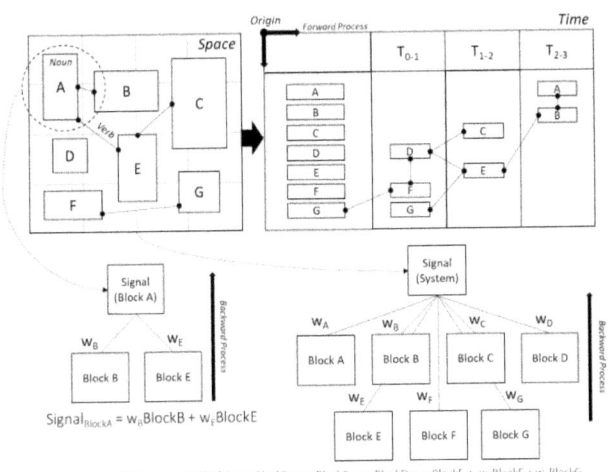

Systems Thinking

Dark Ocean
VUCA Intensity Level (IL)

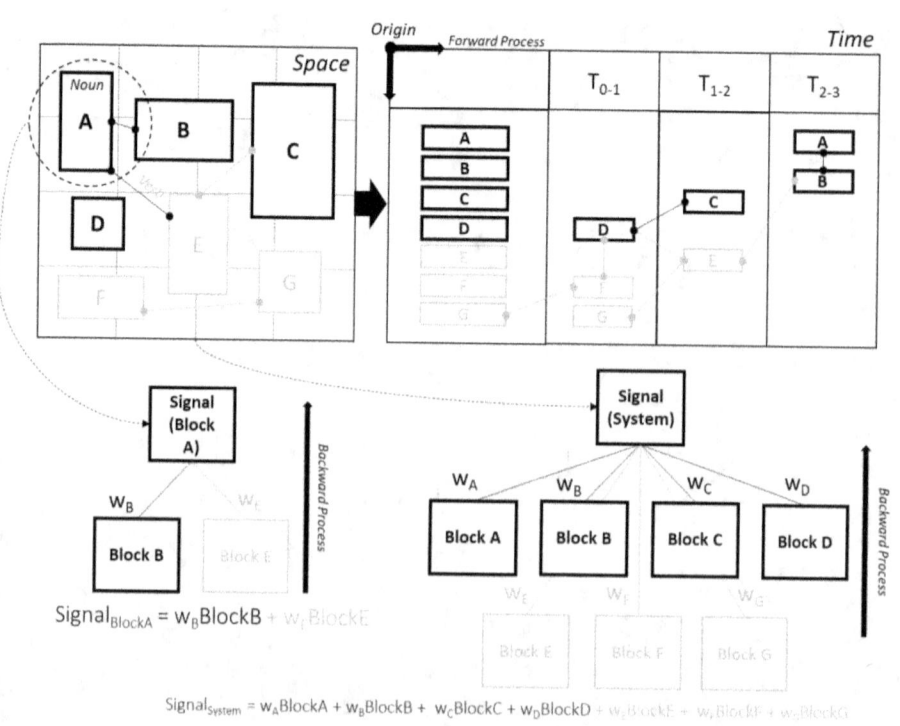

Systems Thinking

Dark Ocean

VUCA Intensity Level (IL)

Signal of VUCA Intensity Level (IL) =
    A. Volatility Level +
    B. Uncertainty Level +
    C. Complexity Level +
    D. Ambiguity Level

Time Dimension:
- Past (T_0) activity/transaction/result/opportunity
- Current (T_1) activity/transaction/result/opportunity
- Future (T_2, T_3) activity/transaction/result/opportunity

Leadership Dimension (optional):
- Vision
- Understanding
- Clarity
- Adaptability

Systems Thinking

Dark Ocean Strategy (DOS)
Evaluating and managing across several business situations (oceans)

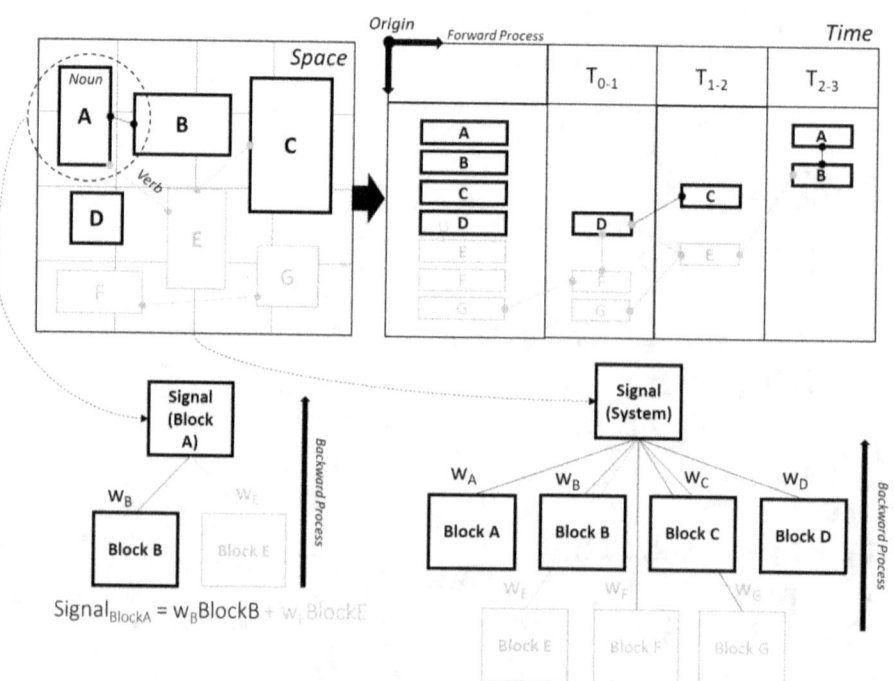

Systems Thinking

Dark Ocean Strategy (DOS)

Evaluating and managing across several business situations (oceans)

Signal of DOS for business =
        A. Success Dimension +
        B. Purpose Dimension (Business) +
        C. Environment Dimension +
        E. Situation Dimension

When: Situation Dimension = Signal of VUCA Intensity Level (IL)

Time Dimension:
- Past (T_0) activity/transaction/result/opportunity
- Current (T_1) activity/transaction/result/opportunity
- Future (T_2, T_3) activity/transaction/result/opportunity

Leadership Dimension (optional):
- Vision
- Understanding
- Clarity
- Adaptability

Systems Thinking

Dark Ocean Strategy (DOS)

Evaluating and managing across several business situations (oceans)

A. Success Dimension:
A1 – Value
A2 – Efficiency
A3 – Growth
A4 – Stability

B. Purpose Dimension (Business):
B1 – Production
B2 – Satisfaction
B3 – Competition
B4 – Relation
B5 – Distribution
B6 – Performance based on elements of Integrated Enterprise Architecture (optional)

C. Environment Dimension:
C1 – Social
C2 – Technological
C3 – Economic
C4 – Ecological
C5 – Political

D. Situation Dimension:
E1 – Volatility
E2 – Uncertainty
E3 – Complexity
E4 – Ambiguity

Systems Thinking

Dark Ocean Strategy (DOS)
Evaluating and managing individual situations

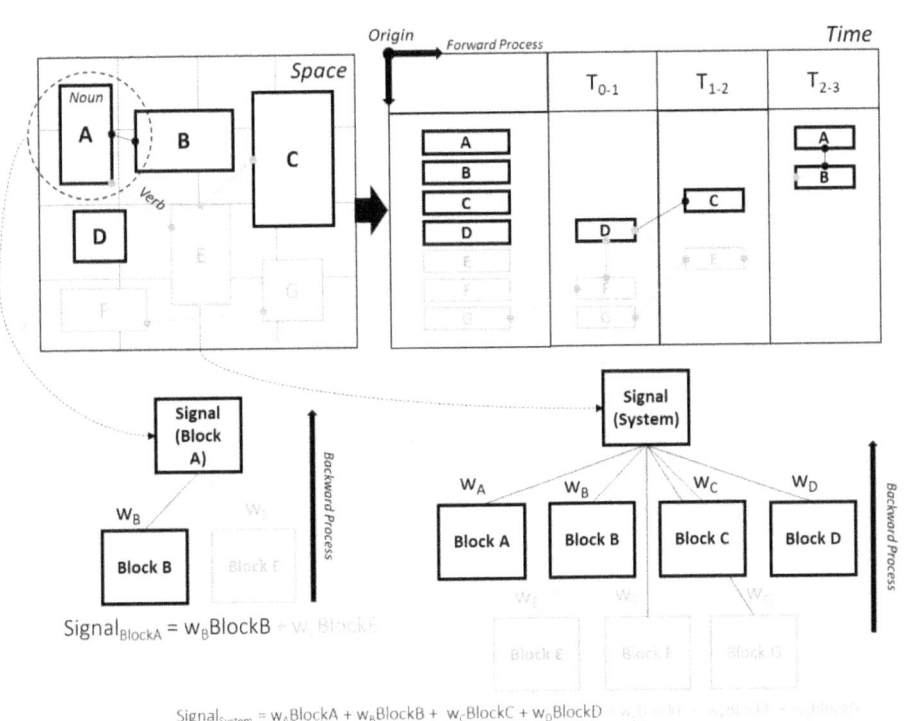

Systems Thinking

Dark Ocean Strategy (DOS)
Evaluating and managing individual situations

Signal of DOS for individual =
    A. Success Dimension +
    B. Purpose Dimension (Individual) +
    C. Environment Dimension +
    E. Situation Dimension

When: Situation Dimension = Signal of VUCA Intensity Level (IL)

Time Dimension:
- Past (T_0) activity/transaction/result/opportunity
- Current (T_1) activity/transaction/result/opportunity
- Future (T_2, T_3) activity/transaction/result/opportunity

Leadership Dimension (optional):
- Vision
- Understanding
- Clarity
- Adaptability

Systems Thinking

Dark Ocean Strategy (DOS)
Evaluating and managing individual situations

A. Success Dimension:
A1 - Value
A2 - Efficiency
A3 - Growth
A4 - Stability

B. Purpose Dimension
   (Individual):
B1 - Education
B2 - Satisfaction
B3 - Competition
B4 - Relation
B5 - Performance based on elements of Integrated Life Architecture

C. Environment Dimension:
C1 - Social
C2 - Technological
C3 - Economic
C4 - Ecological
C5 - Political

D. Situation Dimension:
E1 - Volatility
E2 - Uncertainty
E3 - Complexity
E4 - Ambiguity

5. CONCLUSION

Signal of Dark Ocean Strategy (DOS) = A.Success Dimension + B.Purpose Dimension (Business/Individual) + C.Environment Dimension + E.Situation Dimension

When: E.Situation Dimension = Signal of VUCA Intensity Level (IL) = A.Volatility Level + B.Uncertainty Level + C.Complexity Level + D.Ambiguity Level

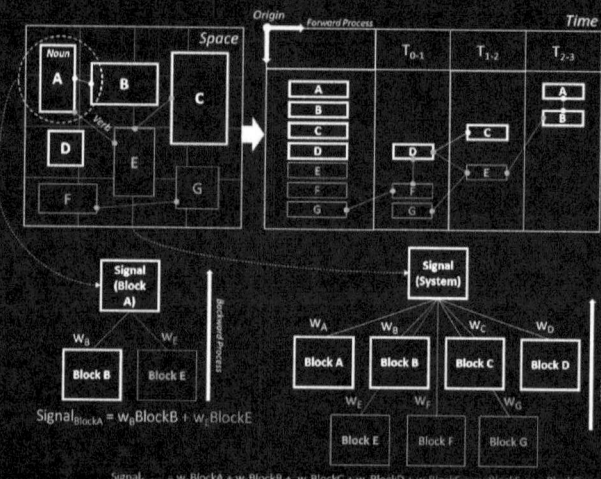

A. Success Dimension:
A1 - Value
A2 - Efficiency
A3 - Growth
A4 - Stability

C. Environment Dimension:
C1 - Social
C2 - Technological
C3 - Economic
C4 - Ecological
C5 - Political

D. Situation Dimension:
E1 - Volatility
E2 - Uncertainty
E3 - Complexity
E4 - Ambiguity

B. Purpose Dimension (Business):
B1 - Production
B2 - Satisfaction
B3 - Competition
B4 - Relation
B5 - Distribution
B6 - Performance based on elements of Integrated Enterprise Architecture (optional)

B. Purpose Dimension (Individual):
B1 - Education
B2 - Satisfaction
B3 - Competition
B4 - Relation
B5 - Performance based on elements of Integrated Life Architecture (optional)

6. REFERENCE

[1] DLTM: Describe Less Think More

[2] Integrated Enterprise Architecture

[3] Integrated Life Architecture

[4] CHAMPSPACE: Living as a Champion

[5] Blank Block

[6] Thinking Series

[7] In Action Series

The worth metrics and systems thinking
for competitive advantage
in the VUCA world.

DLTM

www.ingramcontent.com/pod-product-compliance
Lightning Source LLC
Chambersburg PA
CBHW070246220526
45465CB00004B/1542